Other Ranks – not included

William Noakes

Pen Press

© William Noakes 2009

All rights reserved

No part of this publication may be reproduced,
stored in a retrieval system, or transmitted
in any form or by any means, without
the prior permission in writing of the publisher,
nor be otherwise circulated in any form of binding or cover other
than that in which it is published and without a similar condition
including this condition being imposed on the subsequent
purchaser.

First published in Great Britain by Pen Press
an Imprint of Indepenpress Publishing Ltd
25 Eastern Place
Brighton
BN2 1GJ

ISBN13: 978-1-906710-92-7

Printed and bound in the UK

A catalogue record of this book is available from
the British Library

Cover design by Jacqueline Abromeit

I dedicate this book to Lydia my wife, who has checked and corrected any of my grammar and spelling mistakes. I cannot thank her enough.

Preface

I wish to make it quite clear that any of the controversial topics that I comment on in this book are purely my own. I certainly do not profess to be an authority on these subjects, only that I feel one should take a fresh look at these topics and perhaps not to be rushed into actions on the views and theories preached by so-called experts. Some of my comments come from teachings by my school teacher, which is now a very long time ago! My reason for writing this book, initially, was to attract people's attention and to make them aware of how the current theoretical problems may be over emphasised which should be appraised with a fresh **open** mind. The second part of my book is partly about my late father and then about some of my experiences whilst serving in the Royal Air Force during the Second World War.

William Noakes
June 2008

Chapter One

I am English and very proud of the fact, so that when I read current 'historians' telling me that during the indiscriminate German air-raid bombing of 1940 onwards, that we the civilian population of Great Britain were thinking of giving in to the havoc, death and destruction caused during the indiscriminate German air-raids, then they must surely be living on a different planet from me. As one of the many hundreds of thousands who went through the 'German blitz' and served in the armed forces during the Second World War, never once was I confronted with this sort of negative thinking. Indeed after a night of indiscriminate destruction one would often hear many a victim of the bombing say, 'If that's Jerry's best, hard luck on him.'

One thing one learned very soon after the initial air-raids was to make sure that one had plenty of water safely stored in buckets, kettles and saucepans. It was not unusual to come out of the air-raid shelter after the all-clear siren in the morning to find that there was neither electricity, water nor a gas supply. So with this 'water cache' at the ready, then at least one could have a cold wash and a drink of water before going to work.

I have always admired the love of their country shown by the Irish, Scottish and Welsh people no matter where they are residing. One is often told that there are many more of our Celtic friends living outside of the UK than in it, yet wherever they are they always celebrate their Saints day and fly their country's flag with terrific passion, unlike we English who appear to suddenly remember St George and the English flag when we are usually pursuing some helpless course on the football field. Very rarely do they show this passion on the due date of our patron Saint, St George! (It is April the 23rd by the way.) Again, as with England, I never heard of any Celt wanting to give in to the indiscriminate German bombing or to their troops during the WWII period.

Little is spoken of the fact that during the German night bombing, compulsory street 'fire watching' rosters were introduced which were to be manned by local residents. At the beginning of the air raids large local fires would be brought about through the many thousands of incendiary bombs dropped on us during an air-raid which were not being dealt with immediately. We had ARP Wardens but they were usually tied up dealing with the chaos of bombed buildings and trying to dig out of the rubble people who were still alive. The Government issued a directive that all able bodied male civilians must start to organise rosters to cover this situation. They were controlled by the ARP Wardens and covered all men who were 16 years of age or over. As I was just 16 and so young, the organisers in our street always allowed me have an early shift. The only way one could be excused from street firewatching was if you worked in London, or any large City and you had to do firewatching in your employer's buildings. As in today's environment, people working in any large UK city when they leave these places of work the area becomes a sort of a ghost town. Also as the bombing increased in velocity it became impossible to repair or rebuild damaged bombed property. It would probably have been a waste of time anyway as it was more than likely to suffer the same fate. Instead, a bombed site could be turned into a large water deposit. These 'water sites' would be used by the fire brigade and their mobile high pressure water pumps to help put out local fires. All very ingenious, especially when water mains were hit. Give in do I hear? Balderdash!

An interesting point comes to mind here. Currently there appears to be a cult that refers to the Germans, of the Second World War, as Nazis. Other than for this politically-minded period that we live in, perhaps we must not call them Germans but Nazis. However, Nazi was a political party that was started by Hitler and his henchmen. They were known in Britain as the 'German Socialist Party'. However, in Germany the phonetic spelling was 'National Sozialist Party', so look at the German spelling ('*Na*tional So*zi*alist Party'). If you take the two italics, *Na* and *zi* you arrive at how the German Authority called themselves Nazis. Our wonderful wartime Prime Minister, Winston Churchill, with his penchant for exaggeration possibly found that to call Germans 'Nazis' made them sound especially more sinister. What a man! It is possibly the reason why should you ask a German if he was a Nazi during the War he replies 'no'. It would be like the Germans saying that they fought the Labour Party or the Conservative Party during the Second World War.

I was originally going to tackle the seemingly unfair way that, in my opinion, other ranks were treated in the Armed Services during the First and Second World Wars. However, as with a first attempt at writing a book one's mind is flooded with many other topics that one wishes to air, albeit personal ones. It is often said that history is written by the Victors and not the Vanquished and this is proven down the ages. However, early history was recorded by paid scribes for a King or his Generals. The record never ever mentioned any faux pas committed by these people, so the King or his Generals always came out as brilliant tacticians. It seems to me that this method of recording wars has virtually never changed, possibly under the Noblesse Oblige syndrome in the UK. So when one reads the 'Official Record' of a campaign it will invariably have been written by a high-ranking officer without much mention of the ordinary men under his command. These men often get a 'perfunctory orotund pat on the back' as it were but that is all, almost a gratuitous afterthought.

I could not help but notice that after the very last parade in France of British Other Ranks who fought in the First World War there was a rush to record memories and anecdotes from these very brave men, some of whom were in their late nineties and early hundreds, because of this omission from the so-called 'Official Record'. They even received medals from the French Government but of course not the British Government. In my humble opinion all too late. So much for political jargon that ex soldiers would come home from – especially the first World War – to a 'place fit for heroes in which to live'.

I have always felt that saluting any officer outside one's depot or barracks should cease. I am not preaching egalitarianism here. I readily accept that one must have authority and respect for those in command. Without it the armed services would not run efficiently. So within the confines of a service person's camp, and to cement that discipline, they should salute their officers. During

4

my wartime service one often saw either officers or other ranks hiding away so as not to salute each other. Also in today's environment the practice is rather outdated and belittling to 'Other Ranks'. In this day and age it really achieves nothing, with so much 'high tech' knowledge which is required of serving personnel that it now almost begs the question 'should not officers salute other ranks?'

The same goes for military decorations. An officer is no more a hero under fire than other ranks. So why is it that only officers receive an MC etc. whereas other ranks cannot? I have never read of a company or battalion of officers only attacking an enemy-held position. All ranks play the same important role during a battle and it is not uncommon for other ranks to continue an offensive move where the officer in command may have been killed or incapacitated. Also officers collectively are called 'brother officers' whilst other ranks are called 'comrades'. Why?

In a war you should fight as 'one unit' and not as separate factions because every one relies on his 'comrade' to get through and win.

I have also read that, in some service groups, officers are banned from having a drink in a bar etc. with 'other ranks'. How sick can it get?

I do not know whether disciplinary matters are still conducted under the Queen's Rules and Regulations. Perhaps with human rights legislation the services have had to update their rules in these matters. (It has just been announced that the Military and the Government are to look into 'Human Rights' for serving personnel.) Whilst on 'Human Rights' it awakens another 'beef' of mine –

What 'Human Rights'? Whose? I often ask. How can it be correct for someone who has been injured by a person whose house they are burgling, make a claim under 'Human Right's so-called law', for compensation for these 'injuries received' from the owner of the house when caught in the act of burglary? Surely, this 'Human Rights' law must include a proviso that any person who commits a crime in any circumstance should automatically lose their 'Human Rights'. This proviso should also apply to any person who has entered the UK illegally. Come on, you politicians, awake to the inadequacy of this law.

Many of the military rules were laid down centuries ago. One rule that always made me chuckle was that one could be charged for 'dumb insolence' should one not answer a question shouted at you by anyone in charge.

To conclude this dissertation on military matters and their weird ways, I was told of this happening by a friend of mine. It was just after the end of WWII and this friend was in charge of the demolition of surplus army barracks throughout the UK. He had been involved in the Normandy Landings and went through to the end of the war a serving soldier. He really thought it very ironic that when demolishing what was obviously an army Company Office he saw a faded notice still on the remains of a notice board. It read; 'Due to the disbanding of our Regiment a Company Dinner will be held in the main cookhouse on ???? All ranks must attend that is, Officers and their Ladies, NCOs and their Wives, Other Ranks and their Women'. Just for fun I think I would have attended with the Company's mascot, the Goat!

The same goes for Commander-in-Chief of RAF Bomber Command, Sir Arthur Harris. He achieved the sobriquet 'Bomber Harris'. If it was not for him, and the American Airforce, I am convinced that the WWII could have continued for a possible year or so longer. The reason for my belief was brought about sometime in the early 1970s. I was then employed by a British Company that was taken over by a large German concern. Our Directors were sort of 'moved sideways', and we were then blessed with German Directors. The German Director that I was very much involved with had been a German Air Force fighter pilot. However, he informed me one day that his Fighter Squadron was not able to function because they were unable to obtain spare parts for repairs to be used by the servicemen who repaired the Aircraft. This he explained was because of our Airforce and the American Airforce's bombing and the fact that a lot of assembly work was carried out in their homes, by 'outworkers'. So the factories, as well as being bombed, were not getting enough of these items from the 'outworkers' which were to be used as assembly items or as spares. He then informed me that because his Squadron was not able to function properly he was co-opted into an army unit because he could speak very good English. He had followed American Football as well as having a good knowledge of their cup winners etc. He could also speak English with an American accent. He was supplied with an American Officer's uniform and was drafted into a German Regiment which was being prepared to attack the Americans through the area of Holland, from Germany, to try and recapture the Port of Antwerp which the Allies were using for transporting supplies to their forces. When challenged by the American soldiers and was asked 'Who won the American Football in 1940?', in his polished American accent he was able to correctly give them an answer, and was then allowed to pass on as OK. This then allowed his regiment to pass through the American defences.

So with a snippet of information from a wartime German Officer, unsolicited, one is able to deduce that perhaps our Commander-in-Chief of Bomber Command, Sir Arthur Harris, was correct, after all, in his belief that outright bombing of German cities would shorten the War in Europe. And to think that this man, who doggedly stuck to his bombing beliefs, was ostracised by many of the War Cabinet and other high-ranking officers after the end of the war. As one who was injured during the indiscriminate German Bomber air-raids I take my hat off to him as one who 'got at them' for me and other unfortunate civilians injured during the indiscriminate German bombing. After the war he was virtually 'airbrushed' out of any sort of recognition for his part in the downfall of the Germans during the Second World War.

Currently (2006) one is hearing so much about 'global warming' and its consequences. How we, of this planet, are racing it to a relatively early demise. However, at the same time scientists have informed us that some 12,000–15,000 years ago we were coming out of an ice age. At that time there were very few people on the planet, so no damage to the environment here – no cars, power stations, acid rain and all of the many things that we are warned about which damages our environment. Surely this begs the question, 'what caused this sudden global warming 12,000–15,000 years ago?' Could it be that this planet of ours has always been in a volatile situation all of its life? Yes, one must look at our responsibilities in respect of our planet and stop practices that can really harm it, but this planet is millions of years old, so we are told, and must surely have gone through many changes during this time without our assistance.

I was at school during the early 1930s and recall an incident whilst learning of the outer areas of the earth's oxygen and how at the outer end of the earth's pull of gravity, small tears can occur in the oxygen's belt. The surname of the largest chap in our class was, believe it or not, Littlejohn. Our form master asked him 'if he could fall through these tears' and he answered, 'No, Sir.' 'Why not?' asked our form master. 'Because of the pull of gravity Sir,' he said.

'Pity!' replied our master. He then continued to inform us that without these 'tears' the build up of escaping gases from our earth would turn our world into a Turkish Bath, 'experts' now call it a 'greenhouse effect'. These gases, some of which we now harness and call 'natural gas' have been escaping through our Earth's crust since it's formation. Later, our form master took us to a local slow moving river and pointed out small bubbles curling up from the river bed. Some lads thought they were bubbles made by fish. 'Rubbish,' replied our master, 'fish do not breathe oxygen in and out the same as humans – these are gases escaping into our atmosphere.' In fact he told us these gases escape through mountains and from the sea bed and have done so since time began. I was taught this nearly 70 years ago and I still have a belief in his teachings.

Whilst on this 'greenhouse effect' subject, I have yet to be convinced of our government's taxing policy in support of their reasoning about the 'greenhouse effect' and that their taxes will 'save the world' from the 'greenhouse effect' disaster. Taxes will not of themselves help in this instance. Increase government coffers more than likely. (There will be some people who will say to me that 'I do not know, or have not heard, that the world is round', utter bilge is my answer!) We are informed that these taxes are a logical solution to this problem. I once read a definition of the word logic. It goes as follows: 'Logic is the ability to come to the wrong conclusion, with confidence'. To confirm this definition the great economist John Maynard Keynes was said to have abided by the dictum 'When facts change, I change my mind!'

One example of this definition of logic concerns the medical fraternities' insistence that no bacteria could live in the human gut because of the very strong acids contained therein. A belief that had been taught at medical schools for many, many years. An Australian doctor, through treatment he was giving to a patient of his, a strong anti-bacterial drug, found that after a time an ulcer which this patient had was suddenly cured. He did quite a long study and many investigations on what appeared to him as a phenomenon. He and a colleague produced a detailed paper on their findings; that bacteria can live in the gut and is one cause for ulcers to manifest themselves, only for it to be thrown out by the leading medical bodies. The two doctors persisted and finally it was proved that bacteria can live in the gut and the original 'logic' was in fact not true. Later it was accepted that this bacteria in the gut condition did exist. It is now called 'Helicobacter Pilori'. So beware of so-called 'logic', you could end up with an ulcer!

Just to complete this 'global warning syndrome, there are of course many other factors to take into account. Again at school, we were taught that the Sun and the Moon also play a big part in our 'climate control'. With our planet rotating, it seems that the Sun and the Moon affect our climate's stability. The Moon in particular helps keep the north and south aspect of our spinning fairly equal and over thousands of years has possibly stopped our earth from toppling over like other planets. I am sure that these aspects, along with many others, have helped to keep our climate fairly even over millions of years. Our earth has been free from our current type of weather change for thousands of years which really should be a yardstick when we talk of global warming etc., not over the last 400 years or so as is the current thinking. In 1976 we had a similar very hot summer. A water ban was brought in and as with today's thinking we were warned by these experts that our country could become a 'Sahara Desert'. I believe that from the October to November of that year we had had so much rain that rivers were overflowing and our water table was at an all time high. I sincerely hope that a similar occurrence will happen this year (2006), with its shortage of rain and water usage bans so as to prove these experts wrong. (It is now August 2007 and would you believe it? we have had so much rain that most parts of the British Isles have been flooded and very much under water.) Ah yes, we are convincingly told it is caused by 'Global Warming'. Ah yes, another beef of mine!

We are currently (2007) going through a period of interest fallout. Money Lenders, who should know better have gone overboard in granting personal loans to people with little or no assets. Suddenly a rush to withdraw savings by savers has taken place with one such lender, that they have over-stretched their cashflow. Cries of 'help' have also been called out by other lenders. Surely, this lack of credit control is of their making. Again some of these 'new' lending dogmas have not been looked at and thoroughly checked. A case, perhaps, of not knowing of the parable of 'the seven good years and of the seven lean years'. And to think of today's view of so-called school teaching surely leaves a lot to be desired.

Reading many of the current crop of autobiographies, I am always amazed to note that the writer has come from a poor background or suffered some personal experience. I did not wish to follow this trend but, to set the scene as it were, I find that to bring home another beef of mine I do need to set out some parts of my early life.

I was born in the East End of London into a very poor family in the mid 1920s. The two-up and two-down type of accommodation appears to be customary in most of these autobiographies – sheer luxury! We were more one-up and no-down where we lived. The lavatory was downstairs and outside, and one had to pass through the downstairs kitchen and then a scullery of the owners of the house when one was in need of this facility. However, we were not allowed to use the lavatory during their meal times because we had to pass through their kitchen en route to the lavatory.

At that time we as a family were four. My mother and father, my elder sister and I lived in this one room upstairs. Some 12 months after my arrival on the scene my mother became pregnant with what was to be my younger sister. Directly the owners of the house realised that my mother was 'expecting', my parents were informed that under no circumstances would they be allowed to remain as a tenant with an extra child. If they did their furniture, very little I can assure you, would be moved out into the street should they try to stay on in this one room. All very friendly! A solution to the problem, and which at the time was a short-term one, was for my elder sister to move in with my mother's parents as this would solve this terrible situation in the short term.

Times were very hard in those days, with no laws regarding 'tenants rights' and with accommodation very hard to come by. (Sounds like the cries we hear today!) I have often thought of my parents' dilemma at this time of their marriage and how they must have suffered mentally, living on a penance as it were with us children to feed and clothe. Unfortunately, my elder sister did not return to live with our family. During 1934/5 she was asked to come back and live with us. My sister did not take up this offer. She always felt that my mother and father did not really want her and she went to her grave still under this misapprehension.

I am sorry to drag you through this but my reasoning is as follows. I was never aware of this 'North v South' stupidity as no such talk about this occurred in my environment until I was called up into the services during the Second World War. It seems to me in our current state of affairs our Government is hell bent on keeping this silly mythical split between North and South England as a fact. So I was very amazed when some Northern chap, whilst early in my service life, began to try to rile me with this seemingly ridiculous myth that only Northern people know what it is like to be poor. We 'down t'South' were a load of sissies, living in luxury with untold wealth readily available to us. My reply was to inform him in no uncertain terms that, 'It mattered not a jot as to where you lived in the 1920s, when you were poor it was bloody tough.' I also made the comment that as far as I was concerned at that time most people in the world had this one thing in common – to have a roof over one's head, a belly full of food and a warm place within which to live.

As I continued through my wartime service career, my faith in human nature was more than restored because one met all types of lovely people, poor, rich, North, South, East and West, and they all had this one thing in common – to beat the Germans and to take up our lives again in peace. So please let us get rid of this stupid North v South syndrome, life is too short and it is a waste of time. We, from England, should all be proud that we are English.

To my mind another trait that seems to be gathering momentum is the misuse of hindsight. People of this twenty-first century are looking back at events that took place 100, 200 plus years ago and making, in their opinion, the rights and wrongs of events so long ago. As a boy, whenever one could see that a decision taken in advance regarding the outcome of a specific happening and then to mention one's doubt after that event would be met with a corny reply 'that hindsight was the best gift God gave us'. However, the longer one lives the more obvious it becomes that hindsight is indeed a special ability in humans. The truth about hindsight is that it is a personal thing, that it is in place to teach us that we can all make mistakes and that with our hindsight we should not make that mistake again. Politicians take note!

To pass judgement on an occurrence of say slavery, as it was in the eighteenth century, viewed in today's environment is not on. (I believe that slavery was made illegal by law in the UK during the 1830s). My reasoning is because the frailty of hindsight is that it cannot transfer one back to the thinking and acceptance of public opinion for the period that is being reviewed viz. in the twenty-first century. Of course in today's environment one would not dream of condoning slavery in any shape or form, but to seek a recompense for happenings so long ago is ridiculous. How can we today say sorry intrinsically to all of those unfortunate people sold into slavery all those years ago? This seeking of compensation to all who have suffered injustice in the past, with twenty-first century PC, is surely not on.

I have some space left for an additional 'global' warming point. For the most part of the 19th century and up to approximately 1952, we in the UK burnt the cheapest and dirtiest coal in our industries and in our homes for heating and cooking. Why did we not have 'global' warming then? In London around 1952 we had a terrible 'smog'. This lasted for around seven days or so and due to the terrible disruption of life and transport, the Government brought in a law which all premises in the UK had to abide by. It was called 'The Clean Air Act' and covered the whole of Great Britain. A special Government department was set up and their inspectors would inspect their areas with special viewers. If the smoke, from building, detected by the viewer contravened the law, the inspectors would issue a warning so that building would have to comply with this new Act. All houses and premises were only allowed to burn smokeless fuel, and the burning of coal was banned. London is situated in a basin so should a high pressure occur over London it had the effect of pushing down any cloud, which in turn trapped pollution and caused this nasty 'smog'. Since the Clean Air Act London has been virtually free from those nasty 'smogs' which were a bane for Londoners and all other city dwellers.

Chapter Two

Before the Second World War my father had joined the Territorial Army and his unit was a Searchlight Company. When the Second World War started my father was called up and his unit was posted to a camp just outside Grays in Essex. On the 1st December 1940 this camp was bombed and my father lost both his legs during the bombing attack. He finally ended up at Roehampton Hospital which was a service hospital dealing with servicemen who had lost limbs. Through his toughness and determination he managed to walk unaided within three months or so of the bombing. It was arranged for my father to be discharged from Hospital at the beginning of April 1941.

Unfortunately, around the middle of March 1941 I had just finished my firewatch duties and had returned to our usual air raid shelter, under a bakery shop, when a bomb exploded very close to our shelter. I rushed out, closed the flap to the shelter and just as I walked to the pavement a bomb fell on the bakery shop under which was our shelter. I was thrown under the collapsing shop and buried under it. After a time I was dug out and spent some six weeks in hospital. So instead of my father coming home to his house which was now no more, he ended up coming to visit me in hospital at Seven Kings in Essex and walking into the ward unaided!

The medical people at Roehampton Hospital advised my mother that it would be better for my father and for us to move away from London and its nightly air-raids once he had been discharged from Roehampton. So some time after we had left London for Soham, Cambs., my mother's parents' birthplace, my father got 'itchy feet' – not in reality a possibility – and was looking to find a job for himself.

Before the Second World War my father was a 'jobbing builder', a sort of 'jack of all trades' in the building industry so he could turn his hand to most things relating to the upkeep of property. It was not long before he had acquired a short-term contract on a house which had fallen into a pretty poor state of repair. So off he goes and cleans up the inside of the house, painting and papering the various rooms. This on a pair of tin legs. I should just add here that in those days the legs were made of a solid type of aluminium, with heavy stainless steel joints. Over his 'stumps' he had to wear a thick woollen coarse type of sock all of which fitted into a leather 'bucket'. This leather 'bucket' was made to fit each of his stumps which in turn slid into the top of his false legs. The false legs were attached to a harness he wore, by hooks, all of which would become very hot and sweaty as the day wore on, ending up more than likely with his stumps bleeding. I think his 100% disability pension in 1941 was in the region of £2 per week so that, to make ends meet, he had to do some sort of work.

Whilst my father was on this job I had arrived home one day for lunch. My mother mentioned, very worriedly, that my father had not yet returned for lunch and would I go and check that he was all right. I rode off on my push bike (bicycle) to the house he was working on and called his name. A few gruff swear words came my way from behind the house, ending up with 'please get me out of this mess'. He had been replacing some old guttering and whilst coming down the ladder one of his false legs had slipped through the rungs of his ladder, causing him to fall and he was then suspended upside down by one of his false legs having hooked over a rung in the ladder. I, at that time, still had my arm in a sling due to my air raid bomb injuries so it was not easy for me to lift him up as it were. Eventually I did manage to extricate him and get him home.

The hanging from the ladder by one of his false legs had not been very good for it because as he walked the lower leg was making a very squeaky rubbing sound. Before he went back to work he decided to try to rectify this noise. The foot of the leg moved slightly up and down as he walked on it. The foot appeared to be held on by a large nut and this he proceeded to unscrew. Fatal! When the nut was nearly off there was a noisy twanging sound whereupon the foot flew off in one direction, large springs in another and an assortment of smaller springs and bolts sliding out onto the floor. I fell about laughing, much to my father's chagrin. It was never a good idea to laugh at my father's follies. Luckily he had a spare leg so we set to, over that evening, trying to reassemble this leg's foot. This we achieved after much strong language and we were both pleased because this rubbing noise was no longer coming from the false foot when he walked on it.

At about this time my father was summoned to an assessment clinic in Cambridge. It appeared that being a holder of a 100% disability pension he was to be assessed each year to assure the powers-that-be that he was still eligible for his 100% pension. He was not aware of this when he set out for Cambridge. To get to Cambridge from Soham entailed a long and arduous bus journey which had to be paid for by my father. On his arrival at the clinic he was taken into a small room which had a sort of low footstool. He was asked to see if he could climb over this. Also in this room was a large pair of step ladders. My father walked over to these, set them up and proceeded to go up and down them a couple of times. He then asked the people why he had been dragged into Cambridge just to walk over a small footstool. They informed him quite solemnly that they had to assess him to assure the powers-that-be that he was still entitled to this 100% pension. He calmly replaced the step ladder and then informed the assembled committee quite firmly not to bother him again and he would be quite pleased to let them know when he grew a new set of legs! Such was the way of 1941 and the indiscriminate German bombing.

Later the next year I was called up into the Royal Air Force. I had joined the Air Training Core (ATC) during 1941 and had attended Soham's ATC's School learning about being an 'Observer', later to be called 'Navigator'. This entailed learning how to plot an aerial course from A to B as it were. After a year or so we had to attend, I think, Marshall's Aerodrome in Cambridge to take a test, plotting a course between the 'Drome', the Wash across to the Wye and back to Cambridge.

Luckily for my friend and I the weather was atrocious when we arrived. The chap in charge, who was to follow our course, was pleased to be informed that there would be no flying that day. Luckily for us he marked our papers as perfect which gave me passage into the Royal Air Force.

At my medical examination at Cardigan it was discovered that I had 'acute astigmatism' and therefore could not become Air Crew. A polite way of telling me that I was 'cross-eyed'.

After returning to my billet feeling low, I was informed that the CO wished to see me. On entering his 'Holy of Holies' office he said, 'Damn bad show, Noakes. Do you still wish to join the Air Force?' he asked. 'Yes please,' I replied, whereupon he asked, 'Would you like to become a Flight Mechanic?' It sounded like flying to me and I readily replied, 'Yes Please!'

'Come alonga me,' he said, so I went 'alonga' him to one of the large hangars at Cardigan. There were large benches arranged along the length of the hangar, loaded with odd bits of metal, and the CO told me to wait by the door. He spoke to a Sergeant at the first bench then came back to me and said, 'I'll be watching your progress, Noakes, now go over to the Sergeant that I was speaking to and he will fill you in with the details.'

I thanked the CO and walked over to the Sergeant who informed me that 'the course costs £600 and they cram a two-year course into four months. Are you interested?' he asked. 'Yes,' I replied. I later learned that the pieces of metal on the benches were in fact parts of car engines and one was supposed to have had some knowledge of them to get onto this Aero Engine course. Before one could take this Engine Fitter's Course one had to go through a six-week infantry training course. I was therefore transferred from the fellows who were going on to further navigator's training courses, to take my place with 'ground crews' and this army training course.

Originally, the army was supposed to defend aerodromes but when the French Nation had nearly ceased fighting Germany we had to retreat from France, (the French signed an Armistice mid June 1940 with Germany) quite reasonably the British Army had enough on their plate with the rearguard action that was taking place, for them to defend aerodromes. So obviously the Airforce had to take on the defence of Aerodromes. So the RAF Regiment was formed for this task. Because the Airforce was not equipped for this training of infantry matters, army personnel (NCOs) were transferred to the RAF Regiment. So along with other ground crews I was posted to Skegness for this 6 weeks' training. The least said about this the better as far as I am concerned.

After this 6 weeks' training I was posted to Croydon Aerodrome to get experience of squadron systems etc. I was given the task of working with an experienced engine fitter and acting as a sort of a 'gofer' for him. The chap I was assigned to was a very nice fellow, in fact one of the people who had passed his exams at the RAF Station Halton before the war. My time with this unit was very useful to me when later I was posted to Blackpool (Lytham St Annes) training school, in a pool of about 190 people.

After passing out as an AC1, I had various postings and with 'D' day around the corner I was posted to an active Squadron. I joined No.1 Fighter Squadron at North Weald half way through April 1944. I was posted to the Squadron to get practical experience on Typhoons. I was originally with No.2 Tactical Airforce, living under canvas at Hurn Aerodrome ready for 'D' day and a landing in France as an advance fighter Squadron. Although I was working on the Squadron's Typhoons the

22

Engineering Officer felt that I, among other new flight mechanics to the Squadron, should get first-hand working knowledge of Typhoons in a less hectic environment and rejoin them later in May.

I was then posted to No.1 Squadron which had just converted from Typhoons to Spitfire Mk9's. Having been in the Airforce for well over one year, I felt that this was par for the course. On arrival at North Weald I was directed to the billets allocated to the Squadron and parked my kit and bicycle beside an empty bed. I made my way down to the flights and finally located the Admin Sergeant. I reported that I had been posted to No.1, handed over my papers and enquired to which flight I should report. I would point out that the flight area looked as if a bomb had just hit it, with equipment scattered about and the ground crews ambling around and the Sergeant not looking too pleased. He looked hard at me and asked me where I lived. 'Ilford,' I told him, then he said, 'Bugger off and come back next Monday.' During my time in the Air Force I had learned not to argue and did as I was told.

I reported back early on the Monday and entered the billet where I had left my kit to find the whole billet had been cleared and my kit with it. I was not aware at this time that the Squadron was moving to Predannack, Cornwall. I thought I would check the other billets and found them empty as well. On leaving the last one a jeep pulled up and out climbed a corporal. 'What the hell are you doing here?' he asked. I replied that I had been told to check and make sure that all of the billets were clear. As time was pressing he told me to 'get into the bloody jeep' whereupon we sped off to North Weald Railway Station just in time to board the train for Helston. And that was my introduction to No.1 Fighter Squadron.

On arrival at Predannack I finally caught up with my kit and grabbed a bunk in one of the billets. I did not know anyone in the Squadron and my appearance in this billet was not to the occupants' liking. One had learned that in the Airforce one could be plucked out of a Squadron, given a railway ticket, a travel warrant and a destination and then left to your own devices on how to get to your new posting, no transport to the nearest railway station just pick up your kit and walk and the same on arrival at the new posting. At your new posting there was never a welcoming party ready to show you to a bunk and introduce you to all and sundry!

I quickly sorted out the Admin Sergeant who directed me to a Flight Sergeant Clarke (Chiefy Clarke) who was in charge of the flights, and was then officially accepted into the Squadron. I found that I had chosen a billet full of 'Sparks' (electricians), Radio Mechs. and Admin wallahs, so my first couple of days I felt out of things. It all changed when a 'Taffy' Lewis, one of the bods on my flight (A Flight) came up to me and asked me where I lived. 'I come from Ilford,' I replied. 'Well, there's a coincidence isn't it?' he said. 'We 'ave another fellow y'ere from Ilford name of John Tack – do you know him?' 'Well no,' I said, whereupon he took me over to John and introduced us to one another.

I soon moved my kit in with the rest of the flight mechanics. I had not worked on 'Spits' but I was soon in the swim of things because the Squadron was flying sorties every day and all day long. During the war we were living under double summer time and it never seemed to get dark! With no time off, other than if your flight was on late turn, which meant you went off for something to eat at about 8.30 pm and were allowed to return to your billet. After about four weeks of this the fellows got a bit shirty and staged a sort of 'strike' without its post-war connotations. We negotiated a system of one day off in eight with the NCOs, albeit the day off coincided with your all night rota after going to a late breakfast. We may have been tired but at least we could get our dirty linen to the laundry and if lucky find a cold shower somewhere in the camp Admin block.

The Squadron at this time was very active and many flights were made, some protecting shipping from Dornier Bombers over the Atlantic Ocean and others far into France and along the French northern coastline. The Pilots shot up trains, small ships and any military vehicles that were unlucky enough to be spotted by them. So we ground crews were kept very busy servicing, refuelling and repairing aircraft all day long and into the night where necessary.

At the same time as my arrival, a new CO also joined the Squadron. He was Squadron Leader Henry Lardner-Burke. I got the feeling that the NCOs were not too keen on him. As I was a 'new boy' I was allocated his kite JX B. Sort of 'take it or else' proposition! JX was No.1 Squadron's identity marking and the 'B' the actual aircraft's identity letter. Some time late in May '44 we were on early turn which meant you took an early evening meal, having been on the flights all day, and reported back to the flights at approx. 8.30 pm. You then remained on duty throughout the night and were up at about 5 am to prepare the kites (Spitfires) for any early morning sorties. One could be called out at any time during the night to fit or change drop tanks or assist armourers to load 500lb bombs. Sometimes one could be called out on more than one occasion during the night to swap one drop tank for another. On this particular morning we had fitted 45 gallon drop tanks to the aircraft. They were in the shape of a large aluminium cigar holder. As part of one's daily checks whilst you were running up the aircraft you switched on the drop tank petrol supply and then turned off the main tank petrol supply. You gave it a good belt of the throttle to check that the petrol take-up from the drop tank was OK and then switched back to the main petrol tank and then turned off the drop tank supply continuing your other tests. After you had dealt with all of the other aircraft, usually 20 odd 'Spits', you then drove the petrol bowser to all of the aircraft and topped up both petrol tanks, the main and the drop tank.

This particular morning the CO was taking out a flight of 4 aircraft. I helped strap him into the 'Spit' got him started and away he went. We saw them take off and returned to the ground crew room. Within a couple of minutes a Corporal Heffernan (I think that was his name) came up to me and informed me that the CO was in some sort of trouble and he had asked for me to see him in. I flagged him into the bay and signalled for him to switch off the engine. He responded by waving me up onto the wing beside the cockpit and informed me in no uncertain terms that I had 'bloody well sent him up without any petrol in the drop tank!' He then proceeded to go through the drop tank routine and then checked his watch. Within 30 seconds or so a red light came on in the cockpit which was a warning that you were out of petrol. He quickly returned to main tank, cut the engine and climbed out. I jumped off the main plane and looked under the 'Spit' and saw that the drop tank was buckled. I said to him,

'You have bloody well hit something.' He certainly was furious, to say the least, informing me that I was on a charge for endangering an aircraft as well as a pilot by not filling the drop tank with petrol.

It was about 6 am, Station Admin was some 3 miles or so away and not yet open for business. So he grabbed the kite's (Aircraft) B's Form 700 and took it into his office. Form 700 was a sort of history log book of the aircraft including the daily servicing, and how much petrol/oil, cannon shells were used etc., which one had to sign after each job you had dealt with and I had signed up that morning as the one who had filled the CO's aircraft with petrol. Whilst at school one is taught many subjects which one feels are a waste of time. How wrong can you be! I sat in the crew room knowing that I had topped up both tanks, so what could have gone wrong? In my mind I went over the buckled tank and thought he could not have hit it on take-off as the tank was way above the lowest point of the propeller. Then I thought 'atmospheric pressure!'

At school we had to prove that an atmospheric pressure of approx. 14.7 lbs per square inch was on us from within as well as without. As a practical test we had obtained a large 5 gallon drum and brought it into the science room. We had put in a little water and brought it to the boil. The science master then stuck in the cork bung and allowed the drum to cool and as it did a vacuum formed inside and the drum imploded. I then thought that a vacuum must have formed inside the drop tank and that was why the drop tank had buckled. If the air-vent had become blocked a vacuum would form and the tank would collapse.

I explained my theory to Cpl. Heffernan and volunteered to talk to the CO. 'You are in enough trouble,' he said, 'I will tell him that you think that you have worked out what has happened.' And so Squadron Leader Lardner-Burke armed with the Form 700 and Corporal Heffernan came out with me to kite 'B' whereupon I undid the drop tank's filler cap to hear a welcome hiss of air going into the tank. I popped my finger into the tank and felt the wet petrol. Standing back smugly I asked the CO to do the same. He was amazed and apologised to me profusely, asking how could this happen. I told him that each drop tank should be tested before delivery to the flights to make sure that the vent was not blocked. A bitumastic was used to seal the plate housing the vent and the petrol supply pipe and it was later proved that the bitumastic had indeed blocked the vent.

Squadron serviceability was most sacrosanct as far as the Air Force was concerned. Two aircraft having to return from an operational flight and in this instance no single aircraft being allowed to return to base unescorted, would not have gone down very well with Group Command. So the CO was able to supply a good reason that did not reflect on the Squadron's Aircraft Serviceability. Thereafter, to the chagrin of 'Chiefy Clarke', whenever something was not quite up to scratch on the CO's kite on return to base, he always asked me to look into it and get it fixed!

Near the end of May '44 whilst on a fighter sweep over Brittany we lost a couple of our pilots. It appears that four of our 'Spits' attacked a troop train, unknown to the pilots at the time, causing quite some damage. We heard that the train came to a halt in a cutting and that the pilots had decided to give the train another going over. Due to the train stopping in the cutting they could only attack it from its rear end. By this time the German soldiers had set up and manned a machine gun at the rear of the train enabling them to get in some shooting of their own. Loss of pilots always hit the ground crews very hard. However, after much discussion between us it turned out that in the pilot's enthusiasm they had forgotten standard procedures in events like this. It appears that one did not go back and take a second shot in those circumstances. Pilots had learned, to their cost, that the element of surprise had gone with the first attack and that the enemy could be ready for you the next time round. All very sad.

The Squadron continued to patrol over the French coast, with occasional slight damage to our aircraft. One pilot just managed to make it to back to our dispersal after landing and then only just averted damage to all and sundry by switching off his engine. His braking system had been shot up as well as the air bottle reservoir which held and maintained the pressure for his brakes, which by this time had finally all escaped! Another pilot was not aware, until shown, that a shell had somehow or other entered under the aircraft, passed through his legs and out of the side of the plane. This definitely called for a beer!

We were very proud of the fact that we were able to have a full complement of aircraft ready and serviceable on June the 4th. The CO was away very early as I recall to cover ships in the Falmouth area (this we learned much later). We, of course, did not know that we were very near to 'The Day' and was the reason for us to be up and ready. Predannack is very close to the Atlantic and we had noticed that a very large collection of various types of ships had assembled off the coast during the previous day, not knowing that it was part of the 'D' day invasion fleet. We had been confined to barracks on the 5th June '44 so we guessed that something important was 'in the air'. The whole flight was present very early the next day (6th June) so that the Squadron would be able to have aircraft in readiness for any call. Again, the CO was first away with some eight aircraft, on what we learned later was a sweep over the landing area. Now, some 62 years later, one still has a certain pride knowing that in some small way one was helping No.1 Squadron to protect the largest invasion fleet ever assembled in all of our naval history.

The Squadron continued its role covering the invasion forces until a 10/10th weather situation grounded our aircraft a week or so after 'D' day. All very frustrating for our pilots. On resumption of air sweeps etc. the Squadron aircraft were being armed with 500lb bombs on some operations as well as with long range drop tanks on others. You know to this day one is still amazed at the versatility of the old 'Spit' and its pilots.

Around the middle of June we were suddenly moved to Harrowbeer. An advance party was drawn up which included John and me. We drove off in an old lorry bouncing our way across Dartmoor and on to Harrowbeer which is very near to Plymouth. It was a Fleet Air Arm Station which also doubled up as an emergency landing ground for damaged bombers returning from air raids. We arrived very late and were put in a hut which also accommodated an American Flying Fortress crew which had made an emergency landing that day. We had quite an ear-bashing from these chaps who despite this were very friendly. They were anxious to obtain our Air Force battledress tops, they thought that it was much more practical than their own. It was difficult to get them to understand that we would be on a charge for giving away our uniforms, despite the fact that Americans were our allies! However, they did come to our aid when they heard that we had missed getting something to eat in our mess. Out came their 'K' rations, the like of which was amazing. Finally getting to sleep in the very small hours we were very rudely awakened around 5 am by the Tannoy, calling us to the aircraft dispersals because our 'Spits' would soon be arriving. A hectic couple of hours elapsed whilst we found 'bomb bays' for all of the aircraft. 'Chiefy Clarke' arriving mid-morning, releasing us the advance party and informing us to get something to eat and get to bed for some rest. We did not need a second bidding but our 'rest' was not for long. Having just about got our heads onto our pillows we were jerked into action yet again by the Tannoy 'inviting' us to return to the flights post-haste. On arrival we were informed that we were to move on to Detling, in Kent. So much for a rest.

We went by train from Harrowbeer to Paddington Station. We were a motley bunch in our scruffy oil-stained uniforms, not usually worn outside the flights, bedraggled and tired. We formed up in some sort of order and vaguely marched onto the station concourse. We were suddenly greeted by loud clapping from the civilians and from nowhere sandwiches and cups of tea were thrust into our hands. We soon realised that they had mistakenly thought that we had just returned from France! Of course, we did not inform them of their mistake.

After the Battle of Britain and the extensive bomb damage suffered by aerodromes, instead of all of the services and aircraft being close to one another, rebuilt and new aerodromes were spread out with all services and aircraft being dispersed over a very wide area. Then should one be bombed it would take quite a lot of bombs to completely put the aerodrome out of action as well as reducing casualties.

Detling was one of the very old style 'dromes'. The billets and the aircraft were all side by side quite some way however from the drome's headquarters and cookhouse. The Squadron's task at Detling was to pursue and destroy 'Doodlebugs' (the German V1 flying bomb). For our pilots it was a new experience. Here appeared an unmanned craft, flying at a faster speed than the 'Spit 9', which would explode in front of you should you hit the target. About this time Rolls-Royce sent senior members of their technical staff to improve the performance of our Merlin engines. This they did by increasing the aircrafts supercharger by quite a few extra pounds per square inch. At the same time they increased the octane value that the aircraft used. These improvements pushed the 'Spit 9' from approx. 350 miles PH to just over 400 miles PH. This then enabled our pilots to catch up with the 'Doodlebugs' and really start to shoot them down.

Earlier, I mentioned 45 and 90 gallon drop tanks. The 'Spit 9' used approx. 1 gallon of fuel per minute. The main tank situated in front of the cockpit held 90 gallons. So one can see that the drop tank gave the aircraft quite an improvement on its range of flight. The fitting of these tanks could be a tricky business. The 45s were not so bad because of their shape and weight. The 90s were something different. They just fitted between the two wheel stays and the oil and glycol coolers. On top and to the front of the tank were two lugs which engaged and locked themselves onto two hooks situated under the fuselage just ahead of the wheel struts. Near to the back of the tank was a stud approx. 3–4 inches long which had a groove cut into it. It took two of you to manhandle it under the aircraft and a third chap by lying on his back and pushing the tank forward by his feet offered it up to the two hooks. Once one had the hooks in place, the fellow on his back would then push the rear of the tank upwards by his feet into the belly of the kite. A fourth fellow would be seated in the cockpit having pulled open a special spring-loaded lever and once he heard the pin engaging he would release the lever allowing a slide to engage with the groove in the pin. All right in theory but only successful after having fitted a few. The tank was then filled with petrol after which came the acid test. One started up the engine switched over to the drop tank, shut the main tank fuel supply and then prayed!

A third connection to the drop tank was the fuel supply and this you could not see nor get to when fitting. Only a small peace of fuel pipe projected under the belly of the kite and this in turn had to engage with a rubber connection from the drop tank. The 'Spit 9' had a fuel injection system fitted to it via a Stromberg Carburettor. Before starting an engine one had to prime the fuel intake with a 'Kygas pump' a sort of one-way action stirrup pump and at the same time pump up pressure into the carburettor. You anxiously looked at the petrol red warning light to check that the petrol connection was OK. If the warning light came on, one had to hastily turn on the main fuel switch and trust that no air had got into the fuel system. If this airlock occurred in the fuel system then there was real trouble in starting the aircraft again. Luckily, by swift deft wrist movement, I had learned to keep the engine running on the 'Kygas pump' thereby keeping the engine turning over and at the same time clearing the airlock, something the Engineering Officer informed me would not work!

So because of this expertise I always got the job inside the cockpit. When a drop tank did not take up its petrol supply things then got a bit difficult. You had to 'drop' the tank onto the ground, (we used to ease the fall by placing some old bed mattresses on the ground) under the belly of the kite. The aircraft then had to be pushed back away from the drop tank and the tank manhandled away to the side. Moving a full 90 gallon petrol tank along soft muddy ground would not elicit much help from those around you! However, not too bad on a dry day but a miserable soaking job should it be raining or following a bout of wet weather. Now you can appreciate why I always volunteered for the cockpit job!

Because of the heavy 'traffic' in 'Doodlebugs' the armourers were kept very busy loading up and cleaning the Spits' guns. A great many pieces of '4x2' were used to clean out and oil gun barrels, and it was the practice of the armourers to collect these and periodically burn them. One armourer, Frank Churchett, was busily burning old '4x2s' tipping them onto the bonfire from a tin bucket. He gave the whole pile a stir when suddenly there was quite a loud explosion. It appears some idiot of an armourer had thrown a dud, as he thought, high explosive cannon shell into the bucket unbeknown to Frank. We all shot over to see if anyone was hurt to find Frank, eyebrows gone and the front of his hair singed off, staggering around in a daze. Luckily, after a few days in the sick bay, he returned looking 'sun tanned' and suitably bandaged. The blast had burned his face and left him with an instant sun tan.

Another time whilst at Detling, an armourer was cleaning the gun barrels. They would remove from each

My friend John Tack and me (right), May 1944. Helston

Me (centre, rear) with some of the Home Island Malay people who harvested coconuts.

Our tent after clearing away all of the debris littered around our
tent. A storm flap facing the sea is leashed close to keep out the
constant winds from the sea that appeared to annoy us most days
and nights.

A photo taken at Croydon aerodrome around June 1946, I am on the far right.

Our 'fitters' football team, August 1945. For my 'sins' I'm wearing the goalkeeper's shirt - not my usual position!

A group of fitters with a Dakota at Stoneycross, Hampshire, which we had just serviced. July 1946. I'm second from the right.

The crew om Ceylon (now Sri Lanka) in front of a Sunderland Flying Boat that had been hauled up from its water mooring, ready for servicing. I'm at the rear, extreme left.

A picture of all incumbents of our billet. I am fifth from the right in the second row.

A very 'misty' picture of our Billet in Ceylon. Most of our mosquito nets are down ready for when we finally went to bed.

Sunderlands at their respective moorings at Kogala, Ceylon.

gun barrel the bullet/shell that was in place to be fired next. After the servicing the guns they would 'fire' all of the guns to check that the guns still functioned, then draw back the breeches reloaded the bullets ready for action. Somehow or other the bullets/shells had not been removed and as the armourer fired the guns so away they went. Ground crews were not known for speed of action but, believe me, I have never seen such speedy exits as I did that morning. As mentioned earlier our billets were close by the aircraft and people off duty resting in the billets came speeding out thinking it was a 'Jerry raid'! By a miracle no one was hit. However, within seconds Chiefy Clarke had received a rocket from the camp Adjutant because the bullets/shells had fallen like rain onto the Station Headquarter's roofs.

We were off again in the middle of July '44, this time our destination was back to Lympe. Before I joined the Squadron they had been operating from Lympe when they were flying Typhoons. We shared the Drome with two other 'Spit' Squadrons. We were now in 'Doodlebug Alley' and soon experienced the weight of 'Doodlebugs' coming over. On Romney Marshes, adjacent to the Drome, there appeared to be hundreds of anti-aircraft guns which were to become a bone of contention with the pilots. Picking up a 'Doodlebug' over the channel the pilot would chase it across to the coast possibly by now in firing range. Suddenly ack-ack guns would open up despite the fact that one of our aircraft was near, thus putting it in danger from our own shells. Pilots were, sometimes, reluctant to back off because they felt they had a better chance of a hit. We were also instructed to wear our 'tin hats' because quite a lot of shrapnel was falling onto the Drome, sometimes damaging the aircraft. We, and the ack-ack, did not seem to be good bedfellows.

Our billets were solid brick, quite a change from the Nissan huts one usually slept in. At night the ack-ack guns would be pounding away at the continuous stream of 'Doodlebugs' that Jerry sent over. By now the gunners were much more proficient and they blew up or brought down a heck of a lot, saving many lives in the 'Doodlebug' target areas.

A case in point concerned a 'Doodlebug' that had its giro guiding system damaged by ack-ack fire. We saw what we thought was a 'Mustang' Aircraft gliding in, without a lot of power, towards the runway being used that day. The drill on these occasions was to run towards the runway to be ready to help if required. As we got closer to the 'Mustang' we suddenly saw the pod above the rear of the fuselage, a positive identification of a 'Doodlebug'. We all about turned and ran for cover. I thought, this is stupid, and dropped flat on the ground. There was then a terrific explosion which fanned hot air over all of us. Sadly, we learned later that day that it had landed on a hut killing some RAF Regiment chaps who were off duty and sleeping.

The 'Doodlebug' was perhaps more dangerous to the pilot shooting it down in as much that the aircraft often went through the explosion when a direct hit was made. On one occasion an aircraft of (I think) 601 Squadron came in completely blackened by the explosion. Not only did its brakes not function but it had also punctured its tyres and all of the fabrics on the ailerons, tail fin and rudder had been burnt off. As it landed it cartwheeled nose, tail, wing a couple of times and it came to rest upside down. We rushed out to the plane, the flights were very close to the runway, and with all of us lifting the starboard wing we were able to get enough clearance to open the cockpit for the MO to be able to give the pilot a quick check and then for us to drag out the pilot. Other than shaken up, he did not seem too bad but was rushed off in the blood wagon. We were also fortunate that the fuel tank did not explode on crash landing.

Another time one of our aircraft taxied up to the parking bay having also just blown up a 'Doodlebug'. When we examined the skin of the 'Spit' the after suction of the explosion had forced outwards some of the moulding that wrapped around the carburettor intake.

It was certainly a hectic time dealing with an apparent ghost-like flying machine plus the ducking and weaving we seemed to do when one was suddenly shot off course and crashed down near the Drome.

As I have said, my particular 'Spit' was 'B' the CO's kite. However, if he was not flying then another pilot would fly it. On one such flight the pilot of the CO's 'Spit' 'B' had run out of ammunition so he flew alongside a 'Doodlebug' and with the tip of his wing's airflow he flipped the 'Doodlebug' over causing the giro mechanism to go haywire resulting in it diving straight down into the open countryside. On another occasion the ack-ack fire damaged the giro mechanism which turned the 'Doodlebug' completely around sending it back from whence it came. As if by some magical command all of the guns ceased firing and we cheered it on its way back to France.

Early August '44 saw us back at Detling where the Squadron returned to the escorting of bombers, sweeps into France and raids on military targets. The 90 gallon drop tanks really came into their own because of the long distances that these operations covered. There was a strict routine when it was time to drop their empty drop tanks. A free falling drop tank would put paid to an unfortunate 'Spit' should it crash down onto it. It was only recently that I learned that No.1 took part in the escorting of gliders, aircraft and transports on their way to Arnheim. The Squadron also found time to shoot up the nearby German ack-ack gun sites that were firing at the gliders etc.

In the short time that I was with the Squadron we moved five times and we were always up and running within 24 hours. That showed how efficient and well organised a unit we were, without any saluting I might add.

As autumn came to a close, Detling began to get shrouded in mists with their attendant chilly winds. However, we still managed to turn out 100% serviceability and availability records which said a lot for all of the tradesmen serving No.1 (Fighter) Squadron. By early November '44 I was called to go and deal with the Japanese so it was a sad farewell for me when I left the squadron. Perhaps I should sneak in here and mention the fact that after my discourse with Squadron Leader Burke and the 'squashed 45 gallon drop tank', the Engineering Officer called me into his office and informed me that I was to take a 'board' exam to raise me from an AC1 airman, to the exalted position as an LAC. I did not mind because if I passed the exam I would be paid more money! Suffice it to say I passed the exam. I always felt that the CO had instructed the Engineering Officer to pass me as an LAC in deference to my saving him from my Court Marshall and its implications.

It is sad that in today's environment subjects such as physics and science appear to have been left out of general education. If we had not been taught physics at school I could well be, still, incarcerated in some military prison somewhere!

Chapter Three

Little has been written, as far as I know, about how 'Other Ranks' were transported by ship when posted 'overseas'. To start my journey 'overseas' I was posted to Blackpool in a sort of transit camp. I had spent 4 months in Blackpool when being trained as a flight mechanic engines, so I was quite versed in the way of things as it were. But this was something new. We paraded in the Blackpool Football Club's car park. Our immediate NCOs were Stan Mortinson and Stanley Mathews, both well known English International Footballers. Stanley Mathews was in charge of the section I was in and I well remember the first command he gave us was to 'Fall in as tidy as you can before the "Big Wig" arrives.' A command very seriously given and quite quickly obeyed. Now the fun began. This 'Big Wig' arrived and called out a few names, mine among them. We then marched off with him to another 'holding' area. We were then taken for a quick medical check before given a variety of injections which were supposed to ward off all known maladies which were prevalent in this unknown country to us, to which we were to be transferred.

But things did not pan out like this in the services during the Second World War. I was suddenly withdrawn from this company of lads and returned to Stanley Mathews and his rabble. This procedure happened a couple of times for me and on one occasion being kitted out for a posting, together of course with another load of injections. The 'kitting out' took place in a large Woolworth's store in Blackpool, and one had to go back and return this overseas kit to the chap in charge and receive a returns notice which had to be handed back to the NCO in charge of this cancelled, for me, posting.

Finally, this merry-go-round stopped and I was at last accepted for a posting overseas. We all met up with an NCO who guided us through this check-up and injection procedure until we were ready to be transported to Liverpool Docks. We arrived at the docks and were shepherded onto a ship which turned out to be the *Queen of Bermuda*, (later appropriately called the 'Queen of Blue Murder'), a 45,000 ton cruise liner which operated before the war between the Miami region of the USA and the West Indies. We were informed that this ship could carry up to 5,000 service personnel and we felt that we had more than this number once we were under way. As she was a cruise liner moving into very shallow waters, she had what the merchant navy people called a shallow 'bottom'. This allowed the ship to call at ports which had very shallow waterways. However, when we left the convoy we were in and started to head for the Bay of Biscay this flat-bottomed ship began to really bounce about in the rough water within this bay. We heard that over two thirds of the ship were down with sea sickness. I should have mentioned our initiation onto the ship which was short, sharp and to the point.

I finally found myself allocated to 'D' deck which was level with the ship's water line! A sergeant, who of course was not about to make this journey, informed us 'that this is where you will eat, sleep, drown or until you arrive at your destination'! Like most RAF people on board one did not know a soul. Looking around my heart sank. The area that this sergeant had packed us into was very dismal. I was allocated a space on this fixed bench seat which was also partly under a fixed bench type table. To get onto the seat one had to hold on to the table edge, slide one leg over the seat and still hanging onto the table like mad, and then slide one's other leg over the seat lowering oneself gently down. This you could only do when the person behind you had struggled onto his seat and that the fellows either side of you had also landed as it were. The table held 20 people, and later we were to find that the width of the table was just wide enough to get your plate onto your half with the chap opposite's plate just touching your plate.

There was nowhere to lie down and sleep, you just had your own seat area as it were. And these fixed benches and tables were row after row, all very claustrophobic. I mentioned earlier that I had lived in the East End of London and had soon learnt to 'duck and dive', as they say, so I was soon on the look out for a hammock. I had asked a merchant navy fellow if he knew where I could obtain a hammock and he directed me to a merchant navy quartermaster type person. I explained that I had been sent down by an NCO to see if I could obtain one for him and this merchant navy chap very reluctantly sorted one out for me.

Back at our table I had noticed that there were round iron bars above our bench tables and every 3 feet or so a 'u' shaped notch had been made with the next bar along at approximately 7 feet apart. When I returned to my 'table' I proceeded to try and hitch up this hammock on the bars and sure enough the hammock fitted them. I then hoisted myself into the hammock whereupon the sides of the hammock immediately folded around me and try as I would I could not sit up nor get out of it. It was like being an insect in a chrysalis. Lucky for me my merchant navy friend came by, saw me struggling to get out of the hammock and helped me out. He then showed me how to adjust the cords either end of the hammock so that they helped keep one's bottom from sinking into a trough. He also obtained two sticks which he fixed at the head and foot of the hammock which also stopped the sides from closing up.

We finally slipped out of Liverpool docks on the 14th December 1944 and headed for the Atlantic Ocean to join up with a large convoy. As we sailed down the Mersey it was drizzling with rain and it made a sad exit from one's country for an as yet unknown destination and who knows would we ever see England again?

As I have mentioned, we left the relative safety of the convoy and headed for the Mediterranean. Because the ship was bobbing about like a cork, with dinner plates etc. falling and crashing around from their racks, the Captain slowed right down in an effort to stabilise the ship. Also at this time the medical people had decided that we all should have our top-up injections. I had somehow managed not to be seasick and was in a queue in the ship's sick bay awaiting my 'jab' when the chap in front of me, from my table, passed out because of his seasickness. The medics. immediately hoisted him into one of the ship's sick bay cots, took off his jacket, rolled up his sleeve gave him his 'jab', took out his pay book, registered that he had had the injection and left him there.

One soon got into a daily routine on board and we soon discovered that at the head of our table were six Air-Sea Rescue chaps. They had boarded the ship earlier than the rest of us and had commandeered the first three seats either side at the top of our table. I think it was because of these fellows that I tried hard not to get seasick. When our food arrived I would bunch up my life jacket between my stomach and the table, gulp down some food and press like mad against the table. I would wait a while then shovel some more food down and again go through this stomach-pressing routine. By this time there were the six Air-Sea Rescue bods, who were obviously now past the seasickness syndrome and perhaps four others still turning up for our food, much to the chagrin of these Air-Sea Rescue bods because they did not get all of our meals. We saw nothing of the other ten bods until about a week after we had passed into the Mediterranean.

One of many things that really annoyed me were the lavatory facilities. They were filthy and shocking. No privacy, with lavatories in rows side by side, back to back with the row in front of you with just enough room to stand up without knocking the other chap off his perch so to speak. All very disgusting. Once we were at sea the whole lavatory area was awash with a sea of horribly coloured water, some four inches deep, swishing and slopping about with every movement of the wallowing ship. Some service people had passed out in this horror hole through seasickness and were being thrown about in this horrible slush. Around the ship's decks were large drums fixed down which were for people to use when being sick. Again, some people had passed out through this seasickness and had decided to keep near to these drums for each sickness attack. No one appeared to worry about these poor wretches littered about the ship and one wondered what would have happened to them if we had been attacked by a U-boat.

Shortly after we had left port we were introduced to our boat drill. Because we were perhaps considered dispensable, our deck had to muster at the stern of the ship. The only floatable pieces of equipment at our station were a few large drum type of things which were encased in slats of wood and had hand ropes attached to their sides. One had to grab hold of a jemmy which was attached to the float's moorings and lever up a kind of safety catch, one each side which quickly allowed the float to slide over the stern and into the sea. All we had to do was, quite simply, jump in after it, some 40 or so feet. Of course we had our life jackets to keep us afloat but they had been issued many times before to other unfortunates who had sailed in this ship and which by now were very much past their floatable date. I decided at the next boat drill to go amidships and try to be one of those who would be able to get into a lifeboat. There were quite a few of these and I was soon accepted by those queuing as being a specially chosen one. I should add that these lifeboats appeared to be reserved for officers and NCOs only. All one had to do was to arrive as in haste without wearing your battledress top and in your shorts.

I was once put on a charge with 'being absent' from one of these boat drills. It was an 'order' that one should be at one's allotted boat station, but, at the hearing, I claimed that I was at the other end of the ship when the alarm went off and got lost in the ship's many stairways and corridors finally arriving back at 'D' deck as the all clear was sounded. The officer in charge of the hearing, on clearing me, mentioned as an aside 'that I would probably have drowned if it was the real thing'. Funnily enough I do believe that he was one of the officers who

45

would have been in the lifeboat which I would have boarded, unofficially!

One had to be very careful not to get caught out when a check was made of the people assembled at this boat station. So when the chappy with his list came along and checked names, which of course had to agree, one had to quickly nip off to the front of the assembled people so that you never ever mentioned your name. Once we were into the Mediterranean, boat drills stopped so life took a more leisurely pace.

One thing that was very useful during the sea passage was my hammock. It allowed me to sleep reasonably well, and as I appeared to be the only 'passenger' on 'D' deck with one I took great care to hide it whenever I was away from 'D' deck. Early each morning the cookhouse people would pass quite close to my hammock with large trays balanced on their heads, full of freshly baked hot bread. These were bound for the NCOs and Officers' Mess. Our bread was horrible and stale. So I usually leaned over and 'helped' myself to a couple of loaves as they passed by my hammock. A little later, the same scene, but this time the trays contained butter and marmalade. So, to complement the fresh bread that I had 'borrowed', I had to help myself to some of these as well, to me at that time quite a luxury. I did share these 'delicacies' with a friend who sat next to me, but quietly, away from our table.

We were quite near to the stern of the ship and further down from us was the Cookhouse Galley. To gain access to the galley one had to walk up a wooden ramp then down a wooden ramp the other side. The reason for this ramp, which strangely enough was not because of someone with a bent sense of humour, was for the watertight bulkheads which, should the ship spring a leak or suffer damage from the enemy, could be shut off with their watertight doors. Over the Tannoy loud speaker system the various 'decks' were called to the galley to collect their food. With all of this rocking, rolling and lurching of the ship it was quite easy to spill some of the food onto these wooden ramps. If one's deck was last to be called, the ramps by this time were like an ice rink, with food etc. a couple of inches thick on both sides of the exit ramp.

Each 'table' was issued with four large galvanised dishes. The dishes had handles which folded down for easy stacking and locked into place when raised for carrying. We took it in turns, two at a time, to collect the food for our 'table', under the watchful eyes of the Air-Sea Rescue chaps. When one was stepping onto the ramp into the galley, any sudden rise and fall of the ship could upend you in a flash and send you sprawling down the other side. As far as the Air-Sea Rescue lads were concerned this was hilarious. However, if this catastrophe happened after the food had been sloshed into the dishes and one was negotiating the ramp when on leaving the Galley to return to our table, the Air-Sea Rescue chaps made sure that the unfortunate carrier lost out and did not receive his share of the meal, or what was left of it! I found that on exiting the galley the best bet was to wait until the ship appeared to be 'stable' and then run like mad at the ramp and if necessary slide down the other side. Our passage through the 'Med' was much smoother and our 'sick' boys began to return to our table resulting in less food for us!

We had a short stop in the Suez Canal with many of the itinerant 'Bum Boats' plying their wares. It appeared to be a well organised 'racket' for the merchant navy crew. They would haul up onto the deck, two or three of these boats and then proceed to turn their hosepipes on the rest of them in an effort to scare them away from the ship. A whole load of trinkets, watches, silken scarves etc. were sold to the troops on board our ship. The boat's crews would then take their share of the profits from these 'Bum Boats' on deck and all would be OK for them.

There were quite a lot of 'Bum Boats' around our ship. However, the other 'Bum Boats' would zoom around to the other side of our ship, throw up a couple of ropes shout out the price of the goods, the buyer would then place his money into the basket which was whisked down. The goods purchased would then be placed in the basket and whisked back up. One had to be aware of the fact that the Captain would give a couple of 'toots' on the ship's siren. This to warn all 'Bum Boats' to get clear of the ship. So at that time all trading with 'Bum Boats' should stop.

On the 3rd January 1945 our ship sailed into Bombay and we were very relieved to finally disembark and face whatever the future had in store for us. When we were 'kitted out' in Blackpool we were all supplied with a regulation 'Pith Helmet'. One usually saw them worn in films supposedly to help keep one's head safe from the tropical sun. As we disembarked we had to throw them onto the dockside which resulted in quite a high pile of them. We were informed that they would be useless where we were going and would later be supplied with

'Bush Hats'. However, what a waste of time and money for them to be thrown away like that.

The change of climate from that at home was tremendous. Back in the UK one could be soaking wet and shivering from the cold, (we did not have the protective clothing which is so readily available now), trying to change an oil filter in a force 10 gale with the scalding hot oil splashing onto your face and hands. Although it was very hot in India the rain usually came at the same time every year, so one would be ready for it. As opposed to the UK, where at the drop of a hat as it were, one could experience all of our yearly weather in say five minutes. The local people must have thought that the 'British' were totally mad – at midday when they took to their houses for a siesta, we were taken out on route marches. It was so hot on many occasions that the oil in the wooden stock of one's rifle would run off like rainwater.

Having been an active 'tradesman' on Fighter Squadrons, these drills with periods of doing nothing in Kalyan, just a short distance inland from Bombay, irked me so I managed to get a transfer to a Tata Aerodrome at Juhu, just outside what was then known as Bombay, which supposedly held stocks of various items for use at our final destination. The sole purpose of this transfer was to guard these stocks and we took turns on a roster system which gave us plenty of time to visit Bombay.

On one of these visits with some other friends we needed the use of a lavatory. After much anxious searching we had not found a public lavatory. I then noticed a well dressed Indian gentleman walking towards us so I politely asked him, 'Where are the public lavatories in Bombay?' He smiled and said, 'Unlike

England we do not have this facility but if you would like to follow me I will take you to my club where you may make use of their facilities.'

What a transformation! As we entered this club we were greeted by a cool waft of air, so refreshing after all of the heat and dust of Bombay. After a refreshing wash, with the attendant trying to brush the dust from our khaki shirts, we again met up with this Indian gentleman who offered us some very cool lemonade – pure heaven! We later learned from him that he was an Indian MP of the Indian Congress Party. I asked him what he thought of Mr Gandhi and he replied, 'Mr Gandhi wants India to return to the nineteenth century with his manual loom spinning instead of looking forward to the rest of the twentieth century.' He asked me where I was stationed and I told him that we were at Juhu beach. He informed me that he lived quite near to the Aerodrome and told me that I should visit his home.

I completely forgot his very generous invitation but some week or so later as I was leaving the Aerodrome I noticed a very large Rolls-Royce car parked across the road with the Indian member of Parliament alongside. He called me over to his car and asked me if I was free to go to his house. I was very hot and sweaty from the guard duties that I had just finished and mentioned this to him. 'Do not worry,' he said, 'you may have a shower at my house.'

So I went to his house, met his wife and children, and after cleaning up joined them in their palatial living room. He took me to their kitchen where the family ayah was cooking a curry. He pointed out to me that the correct way to cook a curry was for the spicy ingredients to be cooked separately, in this case in a large type frying pan, and for the meat to be also cooked separately and only offered up into the frying spices a few minutes before serving, otherwise, he said, you will not know if you were eating say a chicken or a cat! All very enlightening now that we find Indian curry restaurants everywhere in the UK. (I hasten to point out that I do not wish to infer that English Indian curry restaurants use cats in their curries!) It was that the chap was trying to point out to me the correct procedure for cooking a curry. Of course this was some 62 years or so ago and curry cooking methods may well have changed since then.

We were very sorry when we had leave Juhu/Bombay to return to our camp at Kalyan. The reason was because we were to embark on the final stage of our journey to 'the unknown'. Of course, a lot of conjecture as to where we were to finally end up had been discussed, the most likely place and on which quite a sum of betting money had been placed, was to 'Greenland'! As it turned out, quite the opposite.

On the 18th March 1945 we were transported to the docks at Bombay where quite a few other Airforce personnel and I boarded a smallish coaster called the SS *Salween*. She was one of three ships which were to take us to this unknown destination. I later learned that she was some eight years old and had plied her trade between Glasgow, Rangoon and other areas in that region and was approximately of 9,360 tons. With an enormous number of names cut into the woodwork by previous incumbents we felt that she must have lost quite a few of her 'tons' to these unknown 'customers'.

We sailed firstly to Ceylon (as it was then named), and were disembarked and allowed to swim and relax on a nearby sandy beach. After a few days we again boarded, with some trepidation, the SS *Salween* for the final part of our journey. We had experienced some dodgy food on the trip to Ceylon. Our bread was full of insects, albeit cooked. These 'insects', we were informed, were weevils. It appears some dodgy flour was purchased for us by some sharp Indian merchant. It was suggested that Scott of the Antarctic had refused this when he shot off to try to reach the South Pole. When an RAF Officer was summoned because of our complaint he blithely informed us that the weevils were 'extra protein'. When I asked him 'if we could share our bread ration with him because I felt we should not deny him his share of this extra protein' he somewhat declined my offer and left.

By now most bets for 'Greenland' had been called in and at last after a day or so of sailing were informed of our destination. We had left Ceylon with the other two ships but were soon sailing on our own and our destination was to be The Cocos Islands, some 550 miles south of Borneo, Sumatra currently held by the Japanese. We were now all alone and we had a couple of 'Jonahs' who had been saved from landing at Singapore just before the Japanese had taken it. They said that they were harassed by a Japanese Aircraft Carrier for some days and it was only the expertise of the ship's captain that had saved them from being sunk. Also there was some discussion as to whether or not the Japanese controlled the Cocos Islands.

As far as we knew we had little or no anti aircraft guns to defend us. There was nothing in view for us now that we were sailing alone and the sea was in the form of large corrugated rollers. Along each 'trough' we could see for miles but to climb out of these troughs was a frightening 20 to 30 feet climb. Because we seemed to be sailing across them the ship had a distinctly gut-wrenching roll. In fact we were all ordered below decks by the captain in an effort to centralise our weight, but when this failed the captain just seemed to sail up and down them as it were. All very shaky. After a day or so the sea smoothed and we were on our way again.

We arrived at the Cocos Islands on the 5th April 1945, too late to disembark. We just cruised around until daybreak when we were ordered on deck to climb down to the landing craft. All so easily said, especially so with this heavy swell and quite some distance from the shoreline. We could not see very much of the shoreline because these Islands were very low and the main things we could see were palm trees. I was informed that the army personnel on our ship had been practising shinning down the large 'rope nets' onto landing barges whereas we had not! The sea swell was quite considerable and with one's small pack, rifle and ammunition to carry it was quite a hazardous task. I started to clamber down to see the barge zoom up past me. I then noticed that there was an iron railing type of structure welded to the side of the ship just along from me and I edged myself along to it. I grasped this structure and waited for the barge to climb up beside the ship and as it started to descend I jumped and landed safely. On its next upward climb the side of the barge caught this railing structure that I had just vacated and ripped off some of the barge's side. All very hairy.

In no time we were sliding onto the beach, the front flap lowered and we scrambled off feeling very lucky. We were quickly mustered on the beach and allocated an area which was to be our 'base' for the time being. We were soon to learn that the Island was the home for thousands of land crabs, which soon took to hiding in our small packs during the day. So when we tried to sleep at night we had to first of all shoo them away. This was not an easy task because they were quite aggressive and to add to our misery it appeared to rain every night we were stuck on this beachhead.

As I have mentioned earlier, organisation in the armed forces during the war was very sparse, even non existent in many cases. This appeared to be the case for us. When loading up the ship in Bombay, they had first of all packed away our tents. On top of these were the various paraphernalia for the Islands and so on until the holds were full. From memory I think it was some two weeks before we received our tents, in the meantime we were moved further up the Island along a very rough track to where we would ultimately pitch our tents. Again we were sorted into 'gangs' of four people which when we finally received our tents would be our 'home' together. Our first task was to start to clear the ground of fallen palm thongs and other debris, carry it to the shore line and burn it. At the same time I am afraid quite a lot of land crabs came to a fiery end. A case of priorities as far as our comfort was concerned.

These working parties were controlled by a larger than life Station Warrant Officer by the name of Bellerby. At first we were each allocated about a gallon of water each day. This was for drinking, cooking and washing. One was neither allowed to urinate nor defecate onto the ground. Our only supply of water was pumped up from below this coral rock and such actions would contaminate this very essential commodity. This was, during the first week or so, very irksome until proper latrines were installed.

After a couple of weeks a routine seemed to occur and we were very much involved in this initial clearing up process. SWO Bellerby insisted the we shaved every day and with the sea very close to us we were able to swim after our daily duty and wash off our sweat and grime. As we cleared some very large areas we then had the task of putting up some very large tents. They were some 60 feet long and about 30 feet wide, rather like a circus tent. Another nuisance were very large black ants that had a bite like a dog and crawled out from beneath the coral. Once we four had our tent erected we went down to the coral beach and carted back some of it to put onto the floor of our tent and spread it to about 3 inches deep. The ants soon got fed up with trying to climb out of the coral because as they emerged the sand collapsed into the hole that they had made, all very ingenious.

As time slipped by I got fed up with this clearing lark and sorted out an officer who was supposed to look after us. I informed him that back home I had been on a fighter squadron doing the job as an aircraft engine fitter. I was led to believe that my particular trade was in short supply because the war had nearly ended in Europe and quite a few chaps had been demobilised. We had been informed that our base, the Cocos Islands, was to be used to ferry home service personnel injured in the final push against the Japanese. The Allied Commanders had estimated that some one million allied personnel could be injured or killed during this operation. It was also to be a springboard for an attack on Malaya.

The whole of this Cocos Islands operation had been a very hush-hush thing since its inception some six months or so before we had left England. We, who had been dumped, as it were, onto these Islands had taken a strong view on our survival chances if a Japanese destroyer parked itself a couple of miles off our shore and started to shell us. At first we had little or no means of shooting back at it, so why was it so arranged? Our unaccompanied journey from Ceylon in an old rusting coaster would have been bread and butter to a submarine, the whole operation arranged so because of this hush-hush syndrome. The consensus was that some high-ranking officers would get a swift promotion with attendant medals based on our hard work. However, this Officer in charge of our unit had contacted a Spitfire Squadron, No.136, based on the Cocos Islands who were flying Spitfire Mark VIII, the Army Pioneer Corps having by this time built a runway for these fighters and also Liberator Bombers.

Because I was experienced on Spit IX's I was welcomed by the Squadron's Engineering Officer in un-crating and assembling these Spit. VIII's. The ground personnel of this Squadron had been very close to the Japanese on their last posting and quite a few of the ground crew had pistols stuck in their trouser waistband, they believing that the Japs were near enough for them to have a go at us! It also had the effect of one always agreeing with these ground-crews!

On my return to the working parties, the Officer in charge of us had acquired a Chevrolet lorry which was a complete workshop capable of welding, sand blasting and also had a small lathe and woodcutting equipment. He informed me that this was my vehicle from now on. I informed him that I was an Aero-mechanic not an engineer. He just walked off and left me with it.

The next morning the cookhouse sergeant came to see me and asked if I could help him. It appeared that he had been supplied with six or so petrol burners each with four separate burners. They appeared to have been last used in the First World War and had 'ceased' up and he asked me if I could clean them and get them working for him. I informed him that I would do my best. By late that evening I had got all six working and he came and collected them the next day. He was so pleased with them that he sent over to me a very large tin of peaches, which I shared with my mates. As with all other essential items our proper food did not arrive for a couple of weeks, so our eating had been mainly shared tins of corned beef and hard tack biscuits. It was quite hot on our Island and one used to 'pour out' the corned beef from its tin. So the tin of peaches was certainly a 'special treat' for us.

It is amazing how, during a war, troops adapt very quickly to their situation and usually come up smiling. Before long all tented areas were now being used for their specific purposes, the runway was already being used and some sort of a routine was in operation. Due to our restricted diet I was now down to approx. 9.5 stones in weight, from approx. 11.5 stones and this weight loss had also affected all other personnel.

So with the war in Europe at an end I was posted back to Ceylon to join 205 Sunderland Flying Boat Squadron. These aircraft had four Pratt and Whitney Wasp radial engines and seemed to be able to fly forever. They were used to carry lots of items and personnel to the Cocos Islands as well as chase up the Japanese ships, submarines and boats. These were very large aircraft and to service them they had to be hauled out of the water. '205' were stationed at a place called Koggala which had an inland waterway ideal for the Sunderlands and Catalinas.

A small craft would go out to a Sunderland, which was due for service, with two wheels which were wrapped in a watertight floatable cover along the length of the wheel struts and attached to either side of this boat. On reaching this Sunderland one bolted through the side of the aircraft one of the 'legs' and then proceeded to attach the rest of the fixing bars to this side's 'leg'. This procedure was repeated the other side of the aircraft. The small boat would haul the aircraft towards a small ramp, tail first. On reaching the ramp one had to attach a shackle and pin into a hole drilled through the tail end of the keel and if there was not a tractor free ten or so 'bods' would have to pull out the Sunderland from the lake. We had ready a small trolley type contraption consisting of a base on which a freely rotateable cradle was fixed. The cradle was the same shape as the aircraft's hull and as the aircraft reached the ramp this trolley contraption was taken down to the water's edge and fitted to the keel with a nut and bolt.

When the aircraft was fully out of the water and up the ramp, tail first, the trolley was used to guide the aircraft finally under a high canopy structure. The Sunderland was towed by a tractor, if a tractor was not available, you had to pull it along with ten or so other bods, and work out in the blazing sun if there were no canopies available. The skin of the aircraft got so hot that even sitting on a wing to work could burn one's 'sit-upon' quite quickly. The riggers had to climb into the wing to service certain components and had to be carefully watched because just a few minutes in the wing could cause him to pass out. All very hectic until the Japanese finally surrendered.

A lot has been written about the atomic bombs dropped on Japan, but no one seems to worry about the American air raids on Japan that, according to Japanese reports, had killed many, many more civilians. Also, as we had been informed, if the war had continued there could have been over a million allied casualties and probably 3–4 times more on the Japanese side. I often think to myself that if the war against Japan had continued without using the atomic bomb and with the many hundreds of thousands of American personnel that would have been killed, how could an American President answer the American public's outcry for not having used the atomic bomb which may have saved the lives of these hundreds of thousands of loved ones.

Currently our troops are fighting in Iraq and Afghanistan. We hear of many parents of service personal virtually 'up in arms' because some of our military personnel are being killed. Claims by these parents that the military do not have the correct fire-power, equipment etc. to fight these wars. Because of today's political correctness one must follow a certain pattern on how one goes about fighting wars. However, the public are asking for better fire-power equipment to be issued now. Somehow I believe that there is an anomaly here, don't you?

Because my weight was so low, on my return to Ceylon I was given a full medical check which resulted in my being sent to a hill station to recuperate, which I think was called Nuwara Eliya. It was a tea planters' club before the war and we were their guests. We had a full run of the club and were allowed to play cricket and football on their very fine pitches. The downside was the enthusiasm in respect of the discipline by the corporals and sergeants in charge of us. The club was quite high up as a hill station and the cool fresh air was a godsend. These NCOs had great delight in calling us up at 6 am and would run us up and down these steep craggy slopes for a couple of hours, returning in time for shower and breakfast.

During my time in this hill station the war against Japan ended. So I missed going to Singapore and help to repatriate the prisoners of war held by the Japanese. It appears that 205 Squadron was the last to leave Singapore before the Japanese landed and were given the pleasure of being the first Squadron to land there after the war. However, on returning to Koggala I did see many of these ex Jap. prisoners of war. I still remember my first sighting of these poor emaciated chaps. Many appeared to be 'lost' in mind as it were and did not appreciate that we were not Japanese and that now they were free. They were hustled away quite quickly and sent back to the UK. After the war I met quite a few ex Jap. POWs, and to a man they refused to buy anything that was made in Japan. All very sad and with many more service men having experienced worse situations than I, a veil appears to have been drawn over the whole of the Second World War period by our current Government.

After the war, whilst at Koggala, we were able to organise football and cricket matches. Some of these were played at Galle, quite near to our camp. After one inter-section match a scruffy short wiry chap came up to me and said in a broad Australian accent, 'Like to challenge your lot to a game of cricket.' I told him that he should speak to our cricket captain and introduced them to one another. The plot was for us to visit their ground and play a game against their best eleven The due date arrived and off we went to this Australian's cricket ground. The skipper and I wandered out to the pitch followed almost immediately by the Australian who had challenged us to a match. Our skipper, a dour Northerner, looked at the bald wicket and said to the 'Aussie', 'Not much grass on't pitch', to which he answered, 'We have come here to play cricket not bloody graze.' All very hilarious. However we were right royally entertained after the match, the result of which escapes me!

Chapter Four

I finally returned home to the UK in April 1946 and was posted to a Transport Command Squadron stationed at Stoneycross in Hampshire. I should point out that my speedy return to the UK after the war was because of the endeavours by my pal John Tack and his father. John's father walked boldly into the Air Ministry building in Kingsway, London and asked 'why was I, (giving my full rank and service number to the bod in charge), still overseas when my father who had lost his legs earlier in the war needed me to help him?'

What luck for me, the Transport Squadron to which I was posted had Dakotas with the same Pratt and Whitney engines that were on the Sunderlands that I serviced in Ceylon. By this time, late 1946, quite a few of the engine mechanics were very new to the job and we were all called into the main hangar to be addressed by a new Engineering Officer. He pointed out to me that as a most senior member of the team he looked to me to guide the other 'junior' mechanics in the correct procedures and disciplines in respect of servicing the aircrafts' engines. He also pointed out that from now on his office door was always open, should we have any problems within the Squadron.

Because it was now a peacetime service, certain little crafty rest days were in operation. Wednesday afternoon was known as 'make and mend' which was a free time for us to see to our uniforms etc. and for us to repair any tears or wear to our service equipment. When it came for us to have any leave time, we used to get an 'early chit' from our Sergeant on a Wednesday to run from 12 noon to 2 pm and take the 'make and mend' afternoon as a free part of one's leave. Remember we had to get from Stoneycross to the railway station in Southampton to catch a train to London. This 'early' fiddle meant that we could reach London in time to catch a train to our final destination. This 'perk' was carried on for a few months when suddenly it was stopped by this Engineering Officer. Although it had not affected me, as the senior 'bod' I went into this Officer's office. At first he ignored me so I asked him why he had stopped this early pass on the Wednesday. He was not best pleased with my approach and asked me why I had just 'popped into his office'. I reminded him of the fact that he had informed us that 'his office was always open to us on any subject affecting our service life'. He was not interested in this and more or less closed the issue. So I just left it at that.

When I was next on leave I visited the local branch of 'The Sailors, Soldiers and Airforce Association' and explained to them that I had been posted home from overseas to be near to my father who had lost both his legs whilst on active service during the Second World War. The lady to whom I had spoken was most sympathetic and told me she would look into the situation for me. Imagine my surprise some week or so after my return from leave I was informed that I was to be posted to Hornchurch Aerodrome which was very near to Ilford.

One of the idiosyncrasies of RAF life was that when one was posted to another station, one had to sign off

63

from every section of the camp just to show that you did not owe anything and that you were not taking anything away e.g. from the library. One soon learned to fake a signature for most of the sections and it was with extra pleasure that I took my clearance papers to the Engineering Officer for his signature. At first, he would not sign them so I went to the Welfare Officer who soon altered the EO's attitude. The EO asked me why I wanted to leave the Squadron and I just told him that I objected to anyone who went back on their word or promises.

Whilst still at the Stoneycross 'Drome' our Squadron had to ferry loads of equipment to France and Germany as well as service personnel. I was ready to see off a Dakota travelling to France when an army Officer who was on board came to the aircraft's door which I was just going to close and lock, and enquired, 'Is this a Dakota? I will not travel in one.' 'No,' I replied, 'it is a DC3', (the American name for it). I have never been one to worry about service ranks. It was enough to try to remember the RAF's seniority let alone the other services. But this army officer had loads of red on his hat-band and uniform. He then complained about the seats which consisted of a long bench seat running both sides from the cockpit to the rear of the Dakota, sorry DC3. I informed him that these were the only seats for this aircraft and that he was lucky that he was not a Parachutist during the war, because that is all they had. I then shut and locked the door and signalled to the pilot that it was OK to take off.

And so I travelled up to Hornchurch which would be the last RAF posting for me. I was put in charge of the Aerodrome's workshops which really was not my trade but as it was for just a short time I did not worry too much. That is until an Officer called on me one day and announced that he was going to make a spot check on the station's equipment covering the workshops. I quickly explained to him that I had only just taken over this position and that I had not signed for any of the workshop's equipment. It was soon obvious to me that this chap was not au fait with the equipment on his list. so I showed him quite a few things twice because I could not find the actual items in the workshops, which covered two buildings. And so after a hard morning's work he signed the inventory as OK and left.

It was now early 1947 which had been a very cold freezing winter with power cuts the order of the day. I had received my demobilisation date and ended up in Kirby just outside of Liverpool. It was very, very cold without any hot water and very miserable. And so my war service finally ended and I was so pleased to get back to 'civvy street' and to start to look to my future.

Having lost all of my youth because of the war I had no ideas on what to do. One thing I had learned in the services was to take no notice of anything that appeared to be 'organised in my favour'. Whilst I was still serving overseas a General Election had taken place back in the UK. I, as well as many thousands of other servicemen, had never been involved in voting at a General Election. About that time, suddenly, one was approached by someone in one's Squadron and hailed as 'Brother' by this person. I explained to him that as far as I knew I did not have any other brothers, only the one back home. I explained that my father did have a push bike but I could not have imagined him cycling to Leeds where this chap was born. However, we were badgered left and right by these communist people and informed that 'we' would win the election, Winston Churchill was a warmonger and that 'they' would control all of UK's transport, railways, docks, utilities – gas and electricity – so that 'we' could bring the UK to heel. All very frightening so we just voted labour. Poor old Winston Churchill must have been devastated. Having connived to win the war, in retrospect I do not know who else could have won it, we just threw him out. So much for other people's views.

After the war I was listening to a radio programme and an Army Officer was being interviewed and was asked 'When did you first have any idea that we would win the War?' 'Well,' he replied, 'just before the fall of France I had fought a very nasty rearguard action all of the way back to Dunkirk. I had faced the constant air raid attacks by Jerry whilst on the beachhead and finally hauled myself into a boat that brought me home. On arrival at an army barracks I was just taking stock of my situation. I was wearing a battledress top and a pair of trousers obviously not mine. I was unshaven and unwashed, fully resigned to some horror when we were told over the Tannoy that the Prime Minister, Winston Churchill, was to make a speech. It was the one about fighting on the beaches and streets but that we would never surrender. After the speech the Tannoy came on again and requested all Officers to report to the mess room. Good, I thought, action already. But no! At the head of the mess room was the Catering Sergeant. He cleared his throat and said, "Gentlemen, last night after dinner a Company's cruet 'went missing'. Now you are all Officers and Gentlemen so after dinner tonight I expect the cruet to be returned when the matter will then be forgotten." On returning to my room I thought after all that I had gone through over the last few weeks or so, if this idiot's one concern was the loss of a mess room cruet, then we are surely going to win this war.' Now, that is real British spirit!

I wish to just add a note here regarding some history of the Cocos Keeling Islands. Prior to taking over their pitch, our task force was called 'Operation Pharos'. Just before we had landed on the Cocos Keeling Islands we were all handed a brief note on the does and don'ts regarding the Islands and their people, plus a short history of the founding of the Islands, and a serious lecture on not to trade with them using Ceylon Currency. The Cocos Island folk had their own currency which was made of a plastic type of material, and for us to trade in Ceylon currency would upset their internal fragile financial balance.

It appears that a merchant sea captain named William Keeling was the first to discover the Islands some two or three hundred years before our incursion. Later a John Clunies Ross became involved with the Islands and started up a 'Coconut Copra' industry having employed some Malay people to carry out the necessary work for him. The Islands were worked on a sort of pure 'communist dogma' without the awful military involvement, as follows: full employment for all, free medical treatment, a set retirement age, high standard of living and a simple code of law. One law appeared to prevail as follows, it was that no worker could leave the Islands and come back to live. So we had to be very careful not to barter with them using a foreign currency. One was able to meet the Islanders and they appeared to be a very nice, hard working crowd, and with all types of work carried out by the fit and able men; some doing metal working, others carpentry. However, the bulk of the workforce was engaged on the growing husbandry of palm trees. Coconuts and coconut oil, as well as the Copra ensured that the Islands were quite profitable. It was an eye opener regarding their way of life; all so very enlightening.

Before we flew our Spitfires, and invitation was sent over to 'Home Island', which is where the main body of people lived, to come over and watch the aircraft take off and fly around the Islands. The reason for this was because the last time aircraft flew over the Cocos Islands they were Japanese and they had bombed them. However, when the party from Home Island arrived by boat, most of the ladies were in Victorian/Edwardian dresses. To our eyes this was quite comical. The Home Island party were driven around in a large coach, which for most of them was the first time that they had experience this mode of travel.

The Cocos Island people used to use the pre-war UK method of using Monday as a clothes washing day!

Well I have finally come to the end of my ramblings and I sincerely trust that if some, if not all, of this book has been of interest to you, then I am pleased. Most of my ramblings are from memory so, lucky for you, this book has now come to an end.